Living Language®
English for New Americans

Work & School

Random House, Inc.
New York, Toronto, London, Sydney, Auckland

Also available from Living Language
in this series:

English for New Americans: Everyday Life

English for New Americans: Health, Home, and Community

Living Language®
English for New Americans

Work & School

Written by
Carol Piñeiro, Ed.D.
Boston University

Edited by
Ana Stojanović, M.A.

Living Language, A Random House Company
New York

Copyright © 1999 by Living Language,
A Random House Company

In association with VPG Integrated Media

Content revised and updated in 2004.

Living Language is a member of the Random House Information
Group

Living Language and colophon are registered trademarks of Random
House, Inc.

Published in the United States by Living Language, A Random House
Company

www.livinglanguage.com

Editor: Zviezdana Verzich
Production Editor: Jenna Bagnini
Production Manager: Heather Lanigan
Interior Design: Alexander Taylor

ISBN 1-4000-2120-0

Library of Congress Cataloging-in-Publication Data is available upon
request.

This book is available for special discounts for bulk purchases for
sales promotions or premiums. Special editions, including personal-
ized covers, excerpts of existing books, and corporate imprints, can
be created in large quantities for special needs. For more information, write to Special Markets/Premium Sales, 1745 Broadway,
MD 6-2, New York, New York 10019 or e-mail specialmarkets@
randomhouse.com.

PRINTED IN THE UNITED STATES OF AMERICA

10 9 8 7 6 5 4 3 2 1

Acknowledgments

Thanks to the Living Language team: Tom Russell, Elizabeth Bennett, Christopher Warnasch, Zviezdana Verzich, Suzanne McQuade, Amelia Muqaddam, Denise De Gennaro, Linda Schmidt, John Whitman, Alison Skrabek, Helen Kilcullen, Heather Lanigan, Fabrizio La Rocca, Guido Caroti, and Sophie Chin. Special thanks to the staff of VPG: Al Browne, Doug Latham, Raquel Ortiz, Sabrina Aviles, Andrei Campeanu, and Alex Taylor.

To my daughter, Aliana Houser Piñeiro, whose love and humor have helped me through this project.

Contents

Work & School
Unit 1: Finding a Job

Welcome to English for New Americans from Living Language. On this tape, we will talk about work and school. You don't need the videotape or workbook. Just listen and repeat after the native English speakers, or answer their questions and then listen for the correct answer. Let's get started!

Vocabulary
Listen and repeat.

1. advertisement
2. application
3. appointment
4. cashier
5. child care
6. classified ads
7. clerical worker
8. company
9. cook
10. driver
11. duties
12. engineer
13. experience
14. full-time
15. hardware
16. help wanted
17. interview
18. job
19. newspaper
20. painter
21. part-time
22. references
23. remodeling
24. salary
25. salesperson
26. social worker
27. teacher
28. waitress
29. work

Affirmative Verbs
Listen and repeat.
1. I am
2. you are
3. he is
4. she is
5. it is
6. we are
7. you are
8. they are

Affirmative Sentences
Make a sentence from these words.
First, listen to the example:

    Simon/teacher   Simon is a teacher.

Now it's your turn.
1. Simon/teacher   Simon is a teacher.
2. Raquel/social worker   Raquel is a social worker.
3. Jorge/engineer   Jorge is an engineer.
4. Elena/cashier   Elena is a cashier.
5. Sasha/painter   Sasha is a painter.
6. Ming/waitress   Ming is a waitress.
7. You/salespersons   You are salespersons.
8. We/cooks   We are cooks.

Negative Verbs
Listen and repeat.
1. I'm not
2. you're not
3. he's not
4. she's not
5. it's not
6. we're not
7. you're not
8. they're not

Negative Sentences
Make a sentence from these words.
First, listen to the example:

Simon/painter	Simon isn't a painter.

Now it's your turn.

1.	Simon/painter	Simon isn't a painter.
2.	Raquel/waitress	Raquel isn't a waitress.
3.	Jorge/child care worker	Jorge isn't a child care worker.
4.	I/clerical worker	I'm not a clerical worker.
5.	They/drivers	They're not drivers.

Questions

Answer these questions
First, listen to the example:

Is Simon a teacher or a painter? He's a teacher.

Now it's your turn.

1. Is Simon a teacher or a painter? He's a teacher.

2. Is Raquel a cashier or a social worker? She's a social worker.

3. Is Ming a waitress or a cook? She's a waitress.

4. Are they bus drivers or taxi drivers? They're taxi drivers.

5. Are you a student or a teacher? I'm a student.

Questions and Short Answers

Answer these questions.

1. Who is an engineer?   Jorge is.

2. Who is at the table with Simon?   Jorge and Elena are.

3. What is on the table?   The newspapers are.

4. Who is looking for a job?   Elena is.

5. Who is at the table with Raquel?   Sasha and Ming are.

There Is or There Are

Make sentences from these words.
First, listen to the example:

	newspaper/table	There is a newspaper on the table.

Now it's your turn.

1. newspaper/table — There is a newspaper on the table.
2. people/at the table — There are three people at the table.
3. application/on the table — There is an application on the table.
4. pen/in Elena's hand — There is a pen in Elena's hand.
5. cooks/restaurant — There are cooks in the restaurant.
6. driver/bus — There is a driver on the bus.
7. teachers/at the school — There are teachers at the school.
8. engineer/in the office — There is an engineer in the office.

Vocabulary

Listen and repeat.

1. art
2. aunt
3. boy
4. brother
5. children
6. classroom
7. computers
8. desk
9. doctor's exam
10. English
11. enroll
12. ESL
13. father
14. girl
15. math
16. medical form
17. mother
18. music
19. nephew
20. niece
21. office
22. physical education
23. register
24. registration form
25. science
26. shots
27. sister
28. social studies
29. students
30. subjects
31. teacher
32. testing
33. tutor
34. uncle

Simple Present Tense–Affirmative Short Answers

Answer these questions.

First, listen to the example:

Does Ming speak to Ms. Roberts?	Yes, she does.

Now it's your turn.

1. Does Ming speak to Ms. Roberts?   Yes, she does.

2. Does Raquel go to the school with her?   Yes, she does.

3. Do Ming and Raquel ask questions?   Yes, they do.

4. Does Ms. Roberts answer their questions?   Yes, she does.

5. Does Ming's nephew speak Chinese?   Yes, he does.

Simple Present Tense—Negative Short Answers

Answer these questions.

First, listen to the example:

Does Ming's nephew speak English?	No, he doesn't.

Now it's your turn.

1. Does Ming's nephew speak English? — No, he doesn't.

2. Does he have friends at school? — No, he doesn't.

3. Does Ms. Roberts teach first grade? — No, she doesn't.

4. Do Ming and Raquel teach ESL? — No, they don't.

5. Does Ming fill out the forms? — No, she doesn't.

Questions and Answers

Answer these questions.

First, listen to the example:

Who goes to school with Ming?	Raquel does.

Now it's your turn.

1.	Who goes to school with Ming?	Raquel does.
2.	Who talks to them about enrollment?	Ms. Roberts does.
3.	Who studies in this school?	Children do.
4.	Who teaches third grade?	Ms. Roberts does.
5.	When do the children go to school?	In the morning.

Negative Sentences

Make negative sentences with these words.
First, listen to the example:

Ming's nephew/ speak English	Ming's nephew doesn't speak English.

Now it's your turn.

1.	Ming's nephew/speak English	Ming's nephew doesn't speak English.
2.	Ms. Roberts/ meet him	Ms. Roberts doesn't meet him.
3.	Raquel/take the forms	Raquel doesn't take the forms.
4.	Ms. Roberts/ teach ESL	Ms. Roberts doesn't teach ESL.
5.	Some children/ speak English	Some children don't speak English.

How Much and How Many?
Make a question with these words.
First, listen to the examples:

English/Ming speak	How much English does Ming speak?
students/ESL teacher have	How many students does the ESL teacher have?

Now it's your turn.

1. English/Ming speak — How much English does Ming speak?
2. students/ESL teacher have — How many students does the ESL teacher have?
3. time/you need — How much time do you need?
4. subjects/they study — How many subjects do they study?
5. students/are there — How many students are there?

Possessive Nouns, Adjectives, and Pronouns

Substitute the possessive noun with the adjective or pronoun.

First, listen to the example:

    Ming's nephew   her nephew

Now it's your turn.

1. Ming's nephew   her nephew
2. Dr. John's office   his office
3. The children's desks   their desks
4. the cafeteria's doors   its doors

Again, listen to the example:

    your computer   yours

Now it's your turn.

5. your computer   yours
6. my book   mine
7. our classroom   ours
8. the teacher's book   hers

Country–Nationality–Language

Listen to the country and say the nationality and language.

First, listen to the example:

	Brazil	Brazilian	Portuguese

Now it's your turn.

1.	Brazil	Brazilian	Portuguese
2.	Cambo-dia	Cambodian	Cambodian
3.	China	Chinese	Chinese
4.	Dominican Republic	Dominican	Spanish
5.	France	French	French
6.	Mexico	Mexican	Spanish
7.	Russia	Russian	Russian
8.	Vietnam	Vietnamese	Vietnamese

Work & School
Unit 3: A Job Interview

Vocabulary
Listen and repeat.

1. apple
2. banana
3. boss
4. bread
5. cereal
6. coworkers
7. department store
8. dime
9. diploma
10. discount
11. dollar
12. eggs
13. experience
14. few
15. interview
16. job
17. juice
18. little
19. lot
20. lunch break
21. many
22. milk
23. much
24. nickel
25. onion
26. pasta
27. paycheck
28. peach
29. penny
30. potato
31. quarter
32. raise
33. raspberry
34. register
35. rice
36. schedule
37. some
38. soup
39. supermarket
40. together
41. tomato
42. training
43. weekdays
44. weekends
45. working hours

Days of the Week
Monday
Tuesday
Wednesday
Thursday
Friday
Saturday
Sunday

Numbers

one	fifteen	twenty-five	eighty
two	sixteen	twenty-six	ninety
three	seventeen	twenty-seven	one hun-dred
four	eighteen	twenty-seven	one hun-dred
five	nineteen	twenty-eight	dred
six	twenty	twenty-eight	one
seven	twenty-one	twenty-nine	two hun-dred
eight	twenty-two	thirty	one thou-sand
nine	twenty-three	forty	sand
ten	twenty-four	fifty	
eleven		sixty	
twelve		seventy	
thirteen			
fourteen			

Singular and Plural

Make these words plural.
First, listen to the example:

    apple   apples

Now it's your turn.

1. apple   apples
2. carrot   carrots
3. cherry   cherries
4. dollar   dollars
5. penny   pennies

Future Tense—Short Answers

Answer these questions.
First, listen to the example:

Will Elena work at the supermarket? Yes, she will.

Now it's your turn.

1. Will Elena work at the supermarket? Yes, she will.

2. Will Mr. Hart be her boss? Yes, he will.

3. Will the other cashiers train her? Yes, they will.

4. Will we be friendly and helpful? Yes, we will.

5. Will the cash register work? Yes, it will.

Future Tense–Negative Answers

Answer these questions.
First, listen to the example:

> Will Jorge work at the supermarket?   No, he won't.

Now it's your turn.

1. Will Jorge work at the supermarket?   No, he won't.

2. Will Ming be a cashier?   No, she won't.

3. Will we earn $10 an hour?   No, we won't.

4. Will the other cashiers pay her?   No, they won't.

5. Will the cash register be broken?   No, it won't.

A Little or a Few?

Say the correct phrase.
First, listen to the examples:

bread	a little bread
peaches	a few peaches

Now it's your turn.

1. bread	a little bread
2. peaches	a few peaches
3. pasta	a little pasta
4. cereal	a little cereal
5. potatoes	a few potatoes

Telling Time

Say the time in a different way.
First, listen to the example:

It's a quarter past eight.   It's eight-fifteen.

Now it's your turn.

1. It's a quarter past eight.   It's eight-fifteen.
2. It's half past ten.   It's ten-thirty.
3. It's a quarter to twelve.   It's eleven-forty-five.
4. It's five past two.   It's two-o-five.
5. It's twenty past four.   It's four-twenty.
6. It's twenty-five to six.   It's five-thirty-five.
7. It's ten to nine.   It's eight-fifty.
8. It's ten past one.   It's one-ten.

Work & School
Unit 4: Adult Education

Vocabulary
Listen and repeat.

1.	aerobics	17.	homework
2.	afternoon	18.	instructor
3.	bookkeeping	19.	interesting
4.	boring	20.	manager
5.	business	21.	morning
6.	calculus	22.	next
7.	catalog	23.	night
8.	course	24.	register
9.	degree	25.	registration form
10.	easy	26.	schedule
11.	engineering	27.	sign up
12.	equivalency	28.	spring
13.	evening	29.	summer
14.	fall	30.	test
15.	grades	31.	winter
16.	hard		

Months of the Year

January
February
March
April
May
June
July
August
September
October
November
December

Future with *Going to*–Affirmative Short Answers

Answer these questions.
First, listen to the example:

Is Jorge going to register for a course? Yes, he is.

Now it's your turn.

1. Is Jorge going to register for a course? Yes, he is.

2. Is registration going to be in December? Yes, it is.

3. Are classes going to start in January? Yes, they are.

4. Is Ming going to sign up for bookkeeping? Yes, she is.

5. Is she going to open a restaurant with her brother? Yes, she is.

6. Are Elena and Raquel going to take aerobics? Yes, they are.

7. Are we going to take a history class? Yes, we are.

Future with *Going to*–Negative Short Answers

Answer these questions.
First, listen to the example:

Is Ming going to sign up for an exercise-class?	No, she's not.	No, she isn't.

Now it's your turn.

1. Is Ming going to sign up for an exercise class?	No, she's not.	No, she isn't.
2. Is Jorge going to study business?	No, he's not.	No, he isn't.
3. Are Elena and Raquel going to take cooking?	No, they're not.	No, they aren't.
4. Are you going to learn Russian?	No, I'm not.	No, I'm not.

5. Are we going to teach bookkeeping?	No, we're not.	No, we aren't.
6. Am I going to get a degree in computers?	No, you're not.	No, you aren't.
7. Is the computer going to be available?	No, it's not.	No it isn't.

Prepositions of Time—*In, On, At*

Make sentences with the correct prepositions.

First, listen to the example:

    Jorge is going to take a course/ evening   Jorge is going to take a course in the evening.

Now it's your turn.

1. Jorge is going to take a course/ evening   Jorge is going to take a course in the evening.

2. Registration is going to be/ December   Registration is going to be in December.

3. Classes are going to begin/ January fifth   Classes are going to begin on January fifth.

4. The aerobics course is going to start/10:00   The aerobics course is going to start at 10:00.

5. Classes are going to end/ May twelfth   Classes are going to end on May twelfth.

6. The U.S. History course is going to be/4:00 P.M.   The U.S. History course is going to be at 4:00 P.M.

Questions and Answers

Answer these questions.
First, listen to the example:

Who is going to take bookkeeping?   Ming is.

Now it's your turn.

1. Who is going to take bookkeeping?   Ming is.

2. Which course is Jorge going to register for?   U.S. History.

3. When is registration going to be?   In December.

4. Who is going to sign up for aerobics?   Elena and Raquel.

5. Where are they going to take courses?   At the college.

6. When are the courses going to begin?   In January.

Making Questions

Make questions from the sentences.
First, listen to the example:

The tuition is going to be low.	Is the tuition going to be low?

Now it's your turn.

1. The tuition is going to be low. — Is the tuition going to be low?

2. The catalogs are going to be nice. — Are the catalogs going to be nice?

3. The homework is going to be easy. — Is the homework going to be easy?

4. The instructors are going to give an exam. — Are the instructors going to give an exam?

5. The students are going to come on time. — Are the students going to come on time?

6. The college is going to be open in the summer. — Is the college going to be open in the summer?

Work & School
Unit 5: First Day on the Job

Work Vocabulary
Listen and repeat.

1. accident
2. assistant
3. customers
4. dental
5. directions
6. disability
7. medical
8. overtime
9. paycheck
10. policy
11. salary
12. shift
13. supervisor
14. time card
15. time clock
16. wages
17. weekly

Kitchen Vocabulary

1. boil
2. breakfast
3. chop
4. dinner
5. fish
6. fry
7. kitchen
8. lunch
9. meal
10. meat
11. pans
12. pots
13. refrigerator
14. serve
15. stove
16. wash

Affirmative Sentences

Make sentences from these words.
First, listen to the example:

Ming/listen	Ming is listening.

Now it's your turn.

1. Ming/listen — Ming is listening.
2. Ms. Chan/speak — Ms. Chan is speaking.
3. The waiters/take orders — The waiters are taking orders.
4. You and I/eat dinner — You and I are eating dinner.
5. I/order lunch — I am ordering lunch.

Negative Sentences

Make sentences from these words.
First, listen to the example:

Ms. Chan/cook	Ms. Chan is not cooking.

Now it's your turn.

1.	Ms. Chan/cook	Ms Chan is not cooking.
2.	The assistants/ serving dinner	The assistants are not serving dinner.
3.	Chef Lee/wash- ing dishes	Chef Lee is not washing dishes.
4.	You and I/clean- ing tables	You and I are not cleaning tables.
5.	I/eating dinner	I am not eating dinner.

Yes and No Answers

Answer these questions.
First, listen to the example:

Is Ms. Chan supervising?	Yes, she is.
Is Chef Lee cleaning the kitchen?	No, he isn't.

Now it's your turn.

1. Is Ms. Chan supervising? — Yes, she is.
2. Are the waiters taking orders? — Yes, they are.
3. Is Chef Lee cleaning the kitchen? — No, he isn't.
4. Are the customers eating dinner? — Yes, they are.
5. Is Ming helping Chef Lee? — Yes, she is.

Object Pronouns

Substitute the noun with the pronoun
First, listen to the example:

> Ming is helping Chef Lee.   She is helping him.

Now it's your turn.

1. Ming is helping Chef Lee. — She is helping him.
2. Chef Lee is chopping vegetables. — He is chopping them.
3. The waiters are taking orders. — They are taking them.
4. I am eating with you and your family. — I am eating with you.
5. You and I are eating the rolls. — We are eating them.

Prepositions of Place—*In, On, At*

Make sentences with the correct prepositions.

First, listen to the example:

carrot/table   The carrot is on the table.

Now it's your turn.

1. carrot/table   The carrot is on the table.

2. glass/table   The glass is on the table.

3. meat/refrigerator   The meat is in the refrigerator.

4. rice/pot   The rice is in the pot.

5. pot/stove   The pot is on the stove.

Which?

Answer these questions.
First, listen to the examples:

Which rice does
Ming cook?
(white)

She cooks the white
rice.

Which chef does
she work with?
(Lee)

She works with Chef
Lee.

Now it's your turn.

1. Which rice does
   Ming cook?
   (white)

   She cooks the white
   rice.

2. Which chef does
   she work
   with? (Lee)

   She works with Chef
   Lee.

3. Which restau-
   rant does she
   work at? (The
   Jade Palace)

   She works at The
   Jade Palace Restau-
   rant.

4. Which check
   does she get
   every week? (pay)

   She gets a paycheck.

5. Which insurance
   does she have?
   (medical and
   dental)

   She has medical and
   dental insurance.

Adverbs of Manner

Answer the questions with these words.
First, listen to the example:

| How does Chef Lee cook? (well) | He cooks well. |

Now it's your turn.

1. How does Chef Lee cook? (well) — He cooks well.
2. How does Sasha cook? (badly) — He cooks badly.
3. How does Ming chop vegetables? (slowly) — She chops slowly.
4. How does Jorge chop vegetables? (fast) — He chops fast.
5. How do the waiters work? (hard) — They work hard.

Work & School
Unit 6: Getting a Driver's License and Buying a Car

Vocabulary
Listen and repeat.
1. bargain
2. car dealer
3. down payment
4. driver's education
5. driver's manual
6. installments
7. license
8. new car
9. offer
10. permit
11. photo
12. practice
13. Registry of Motor Vehicles
14. road test
15. safety
16. seat belt
17. test drive
18. used car
19. warranty
20. written test

Short Answers – Affirmative and Negative

Answer these questions.
First, listen to the example:

> Can Jorge buy a new car?   No, he can't.

Now it's your turn.

1. Can Jorge buy a new car?   No, he can't.
2. Can Raquel go to the dealer with him?   Yes, she can.
3. Can he find very cheap cars?   No, he can't.
4. Can he bargain with the dealer?   Yes, he can.
5. Can he go for a test drive?   Yes, he can.

Questions and Long Answers

Answer these questions.
First, listen to the example:

> Who can drive? Jorge and Raquel can drive.

Now it's your turn.

1. Who can drive? Jorge and Raquel can drive.
2. Who could pass the driver's test? Jorge could pass the driver's test.
3. Where could Raquel go? She could go to the car dealer.
4. What could Jorge look at? He could look at used cars.
5. How much can Jorge spend? He can spend less than $6,000.

Adjectives

Listen and repeat.

1. cheap
2. comfortable
3. expensive
4. fast
5. heavy
6. high
7. large
8. light
9. long
10. low
11. luxurious
12. new
13. old
14. pretty
15. short
16. simple
17. slow
18. small
19. ugly
20. uncomfortable

Comparative and Superlative

Say the comparative and superlative.
First, listen to the example:

cheap   cheaper   cheapest

Now it's your turn.

cheap	cheaper	cheapest
fast	faster	fastest
large	larger	largest
heavy	heavier	heaviest
pretty	prettier	prettiest

Again, listen to the example:

beautiful   more beautiful   most beautiful

Now it's your turn.

beautiful	more beautiful	most beautiful
comfort-able	more comfort-able	most comfort-able
expensive	more expensive	most expensive
luxurious	more luxurious	most luxurious

Questions with *Which*

Answer these questions.

First, listen to the example:

> Which car is faster, a Porsche or a Volkswagen?
>
> A Porsche is faster than a Volkswagen.

Now it's your turn.

1. Which car is faster, a Porsche or a Volkswagen?
   A Porsche is faster than a Volkswagen.

2. Which car is more luxurious, a Rolls Royce or a Toyota?
   A Rolls Royce is more luxurious than a Toyota.

3. Which country is larger, Mexico or the Dominican Republic?
   Mexico is larger than the Dominican Republic.

4. Which country is smaller, Cuba or China?
   Cuba is smaller than China.

5. Which state in the U.S. is the largest?
   Alaska is the largest state.

Vocabulary
Listen and repeat.

1. alien
2. application
3. apply
4. birth certificate
5. citizenship
6. Constitution
7. court
8. dictation
9. employment authorization card
10. federal
11. fingerprints
12. government
13. green card
14. history
15. illegal
16. immigrant
17. interview
18. legal
19. marriage certificate
20. oral exam
21. presidents
22. registration card
23. residence
24. Revolutionary War
25. Social Security number
26. state
27. swearing-in ceremony
28. waiting period
29. written exam

Past Tense of Regular Verbs

Listen to the present tense and say the past tense.

The past tense of these verbs ends with a /t/ sound.

First, listen to the example:

    ask   asked

Now it's your turn.

1. ask   asked
2. announce   announced
3. help   helped
4. practice   practiced
5. talk   talked

The past tense of these verbs ends with a /d/ sound.

Listen to the example:

    apply   applied

Now it's your turn.

6. apply   applied
7. prepare   prepared
8. quiz   quizzed
9. receive   received
10. study   studied

The past tense of these verbs ends with an /ed/ sound.

Listen to the example:

visit   visited

Now it's your turn.

11. need   needed
12. start   started
13. submit   submitted
14. wait   waited
15. want   wanted

Questions and Answers

Answer these questions.

First, listen to the example:

| Who asked the questions? | Simon asked the questions. |

Now it's your turn.

1. Who asked the questions? — Simon asked the questions.
2. Who answered the questions? — Raquel answered the questions.
3. Who wanted to take an exam? — Raquel wanted to take an exam.
4. Who received a "green card"? — Sasha received a "green card."
5. What did Elena submit? — She submitted her papers.

Past Tense of Irregular Verbs

Listen to the present tense and say the past tense.

First, listen to the example:

      begin   began

Now it's your turn.

1. begin   began
2. come   came
3. feel   felt
4. get   got
5. go   went
6. have   had
7. know   knew
8. read   read
9. say   said
10. see   saw
11. take   took
12. think   thought

Questions and Answers

Answer these questions.
First, listen to the example:

Who gave Raquel a quiz?	Simon gave her a quiz.

Now it's your turn.

1. Who gave Raquel a quiz? | Simon gave her a quiz.
2. How did Raquel feel? | She felt good.
3. Which test did Raquel take? | She took the citizenship test.
4. Who went with her? | Simon went with her.
5. How was the test? | It wasn't difficult.

Short Answers

Answer these questions.
First, listen to the example:

Did Simon help   Yes, he did.
Raquel?

Now it's your turn.

1. Did Simon help   Yes, he did.
    Raquel?

2. Did Elena take   No, she didn't.
    the test?

3. Did Jorge and   Yes, they did.
    Sasha get their
    green cards?

4. Did Raquel and   Yes, they did.
    Simon go to the
    ceremony?

5. Were the classes   No, they weren't.
    expensive?

How Long and How Often

Answer these questions.
First, listen to the example:

How long is the exam? (three hours) — It's three hours long.

How often are the classes? (every week) — They're every week.

Now it's your turn.

1. How long is the exam? (three hours long) — It's three hours long.

2. How often are the classes? (every week) — They're every week.

3. How long is the course? (six weeks long) — It's six weeks long.

4. How often are the exams? (every month) — They're every month.

5. How long are the interviews? (half an hour long) — They're half an hour long.

NOTES

NOTES

NOTES

NOTES

NOTES